Peepal Euphonies

Meenakshi Krishnan Kurup

MAN KIND

PEEPAL EUPHONIES
MEENAKSHI KRISHNAN KURUP
English/ Poems

ISBN: 978-81-981690-8-2

(Paperback)

Cover Design & Layout: Sajil Sd
This Printing Edition 2024

₹130/-
Mankind Literature
A Booklove Initiative
Puthiyangadi Post, Calicut-673021
booklovecalicut@gmail.com
+91 9744 155 666

www.booklove.co.in

To my World in this Cosmos!
Amma.

Etched in heart
Taken by soul

Poetry!

Meenakshi Krishnan Kurup

A passionate Literature lover born in Kerala, brought up in Muscat, Mumbai. She published her first collection of poetry named Maiden Blooms in 2022. Currently pursuing her PG.

Email: meenakshikk00@gmail.com

Insta id: @meenakshikrishnankurup

AUTHOR'S NOTE

The title of an Author, seems captivating or attractive to most yet to me, it tends to put me in a sense of congestion. To be called an author is indeed pious! As scared as prayers. I write for not the title of an author but to see a reflection of myself in my works or to say, the most expressed I'm while I write.

I can assure many that there may be readers who would have had a thought so similar as mine and they would indeed have a grin on their face more than once at least from one poem from my Anthology.

What is Poetry? If I ask you.

To me, Poetry is an extension of Life. A profound way of understanding Life.

Poetry happens to most people at one certain point in their lives. Not maybe at the happiest of the moments or at the melancholic of moments.

It arrives only to us when it chooses to and not when we want it to.

The reason I've such an explanation for you all, even if it is brief, I would love you all to once have a thought on what poetry is and what role it has in our lives. Ponder awhile. A lot in many readers for this collection of mine would do.

Poetry blossoms to everyone. A companion to share grief and a listener to hear our words. We just have to give time for either its arrival or analyse if it has arrived already.

Since my babyhood I've had a passionate love for nature and neither my parents nor my grandparents have stopped me for who I'm since then. Whether it is merrily playing on mud or being drenched in rain or when I felt that I belonged to Literature and Arts and opted to study them, they haven't paused me. I have had an individual space at home. Hence, I've constantly had my own perspectives.

This could be the reason for me to fearlessly admire what I love and write what I admire- the aura of one fine evening, the burnt orange hue of sky, countless Sunsets, the dewy leaves, misty mountains, morning hums of Birds, the songbirds and what not from Nature!

As you flip through the pages, you'll know the involvement of them in my poetry. They are meant to be intense, indeed, for all that it offers to me. May this Anthology be a tribute to them- for romancing, for making me the lady-love, for granting me to love my lover just as the Moon worships its Stars.

I hope you all will enjoy reading this as much as I enjoyed penning it down.

Meenakshi Krishnan Kurup

FOREWORD

Meenakshi's foray into Peepal Euphonies brings out the transformation she underwent over the years. It is said that 'a good book is the life-blood of a master spirit.' Of all the forms of Literature Poetry is the most demanding as it springs out of the innermost recesses of our mind. And while some people call it as an act of sensation, others highlight it as a sublime experience. Further an act of versification is essentially the product of esemplastic imagination.

In other words it is unification of imagination. Hence what is seen with the naked eye gets dissolved, dissipated inorder to recreate. Thus versification eventually is an act of recreation.

In this context, Meenakshi recreates life in her own independent way.

Gradually she becomes an innovator, who contributes something new and vibrant.

In this unique moment of creation she breaks out of the shell of her mundane existence. She pronounces herself to be at large, and 'certain multitudes.'

She is drawn into the vortex of creation. And eventually the act of creation gets the better of herself. Virtually she identifies herself with the Cosmos. Now, she is perching on her wings like a lark in bewitching measures of boundless music.

Consequently she disappears into the cloud, an invisible spirit, whose sound could be heard. She declares

'Away! away! I will fly to thee
On the viewless wings of poesy.'

Meenakshi's tryst with words is nothing but an Odyssey into the world of sensation 'felt in the blood and felt along the heart.' And in this process she carries her readers on the relentless wings of imagination. Her thought provoking poem 'Revival,' captures the magical spell of her intuition which gets better of herself. She treads across the wheel of time unable to express

her agony. Her mind overflows with the multitudinal shades, colours and moods of nature. Before long Meenakshi feels that she is an integral part of nature.

She enjoys its refreshing touch across her being. And the descent of the December is not the herald of Winter, but the harbinger of a new lease of Life.

'If Winter comes,
can Spring be far behind?'

The innumerable twinkling stars mesmerised her and set ablaze her imagination. She puts an end to her Sojourn on the firmament too full of milky stars. She aspires to be under its spell for a while. Her poem 'Evolution' is a telling testimony of her transformation. And in the next moment she is in a fix, unable to explain her frustration that crept into her mind. Very soon she is filled with a Keatsean dilemma.

'Was it a vision, or a waking dream?
Fled is that music:- Do I wake or sleep?'

Now, Meenakshi embarks on a different experience of being under a peepal tree. A cloud of despair and alienation descends on her. She cannot explain herself and words fail her. But she soon realises that the Peepal Tree like a guardian nurses her and consoles her and is in total empathy with her. Meenakshi, is equally at home with The Monsoon Eve. The rhythmic downpour of Monsoon, accompanied by wind scatters the seeds everywhere. It is a symbol of hope, expectation and rejuvenation. Meenakshi's fertile mind has a thousand emotions in its kitty. In fact her heard melodies are sweet and we are eagerly waiting for her 'unheard melodies' to be lifted ourselves into a new world.

With best wishes,
Affectionately,
Prof. Radhakrishnan Unnithan. K
President,
Sooranad Public Library.

PEEPAL EUPHONIES- A REVIEW

Peepal Euphonies, a collection of poems by Meenakshi Krishnan, contains all the traits of fine poetry. It begins with a short poem extolling the lyrical quality of 'the cheeps and songs of birds in a Summer dusk.' Nature plays a significant role in her poems. The 'giggles of leaves' and their stillness at the sight of strangers, seen described in her poetry, remind us that they are throbbing with Life. The poet's observation of Nature is very close to that of Wordsworth, the high priest of Nature.

Peepal Euphonies marks a definite shift in the poetic career of Meenakshi. Here she dwells on Nature, its phenomena such as rain, landscape, wind, moon and the perpetual human aspects. 'Maiden Blooms,' her first Anthology, discusses mainly her personal experiences. In this aspect Peepal Euphonies scale the heights of great poems in English Literature. It is to be admitted that the poet has a lot to go to achieve a place among the great poets. Still her sincere effort on the path of betterment is to be appreciated.

The poet's faculty of imagination is freely at work in the poems namely, 'A December's Tale,' 'Song to Sunset,' 'Oh November!'

She sincerely prays for a part of November to be sculpted and merged in her being so that it remains there permanently. Being born in November the poet has a great fondness for it. It seems strange to others. But such emotions are quite normal to poets.

'My Dearest Bloom,' is a symbolic poem. It refers to people who accomplish their work only belatedly. Inspite of favourable situations. The delay maybe due to physical or mental disabilities. The poet's sympathies are with them. She writes, 'I'm one among them, I'm them. We grieve not in delay.'

'Song of a Lady-Love,' gives a clear picture of the poet's concept of love. Love assumes nobility and loftiness when the partners share equal responsibility and sincerity. 'Under the Peepal Tree,' 'April's Reminder,' and 'A Keeper's Sorrow,' belong to the same genre of nature poems. 'Awaiting,' gives the message that beauty exists in the feeling of being awaited. Rain conveys the two opposing faces of rain- its cruelty and its generosity. 'Moon- A Longing' and 'To the Star I Once Admired,' reveal how much the poet is attached to Nature.

'A Train Odyssey,' treats an ordinary subject of a train journey very passionately. The common incidents of life which are generally ignored by the vast majority of people make life lively and worth living. They catch the attention of sensitive people, especially the poets.

Good poetry is a form of emotional expression endowed with profound thoughts and aesthetic qualities. Peepal Euphonies treats a wide variety of themes which have perennial interest. The anthology has succeeded in influencing the basic human emotions. It is gifted with poetic devices such as fine diction, figures of speech, rhythm, word pictures and imagination.

I wish great success in her writing and hope earnestly that she secures a pride of place among the great poets of English Literature in future.

Prof. G. Somanatha Pillai

HOD of English,

Hindu College, Changanassery (Retd)

POEMS

A BIRD'S EVE

The rays shower with a
genuine heat of Summer.
Cheeps and songs greet
dusk.
Lyrical that any verse
penned.

IN GIGGLES AND STILLNESS

In mirths and giggles
they were to quick
stillness seeing
that one stare.
A stroller to often
cross its way by
them, were these
conversations
in a language
unfamiliar
about me?

A REVIVAL

For whom and what
I know not, just an
intense intuition to.
To meander around.
Purpose undecided
halts nowhere.
Those bare tours
in agony, behind
bars, have been
wiped.
Perhaps, ‘twas
knitted already
as time moved,
I moved with it
too.

A DECEMBER'S TALE

Maybe it's the
thrums of Wind
or the capering
Leaves, the Flower
to flower or the
specks of humid
in the dusk of
Winter and further!
My eyes are fond
of you and my word it is;
'I shall love you ever
as I've loved the sunset
of December.'

SONG TO SUNSET

C'est le soleil de l'hiver.
The shade of hope who
knocks the onset of
night and the one of
countless duties.
The jewel of the welkin
whose appearance
drifts in a swift.
In awe with your
dynamism I'm.
Who shows the
possibility of a
morrow on tepid
days…
A ball of fire in
streaks of rust.

OH NOVEMBER!

Oh November, of undying
memories and fleeting
moments.
In the delight of you,
I wake
to your melodies,
I dance
an aura to I belong.
In plenty are ideas
to perform for you
but forgetful am
to marshal them.
It's a longing to
admire than to
grant my wishes.
Oh November,
my beloved.
Sculpt a part
in me that
your subtle
nectar shall
reside in me
ever.

A KEEPER'S SORROW

Watered you'll be.
Sheltered you'll be.
By me not.
Away awhile I'm
yet in heartfelt
thoughts of you.
In our to come
encounter,
will you forgive
for this sudden
move?

TO RAIN

Like one's supper
of the eve are you.
In the midway
days of the year;
ordinary, mighty
and endless.

You quench the
hunger ones or
the roots even
a rivulet in
drought.
Dear, you know me?

I never looked
at you to praise.
You were my
dun and dark.
A ruthless who
put me to tears.

By and by, you
were a being to
have come to
wipe my grief.
To name now,
'devotion.'

A TENDER DEVOTEE

Such scent of it,
pertains in each nook.
Oh! Its' might strangles
when shan't love in
wholesome.
Sprung in spirit of
an eve that mars
in morn come never.
I'm a bloom to a
being whom cherishes
not for thunders lone.

EVOLUTION

So pretentious I was.
I had a flair to keep
lying; to my
subconscious.
On the shores,
I wanted to walk
deep, devotional
and accompany
Amphitrite.
Not long that
I thought no
fragments of mine
be left for burial.

I'm at an alike shore,
my feet gulped
often by waves.
I may fear none.
Among the waves
come shells and
stars.
I had had the taste

of losing myself.
Presently,
I'm making it to
taste finer.

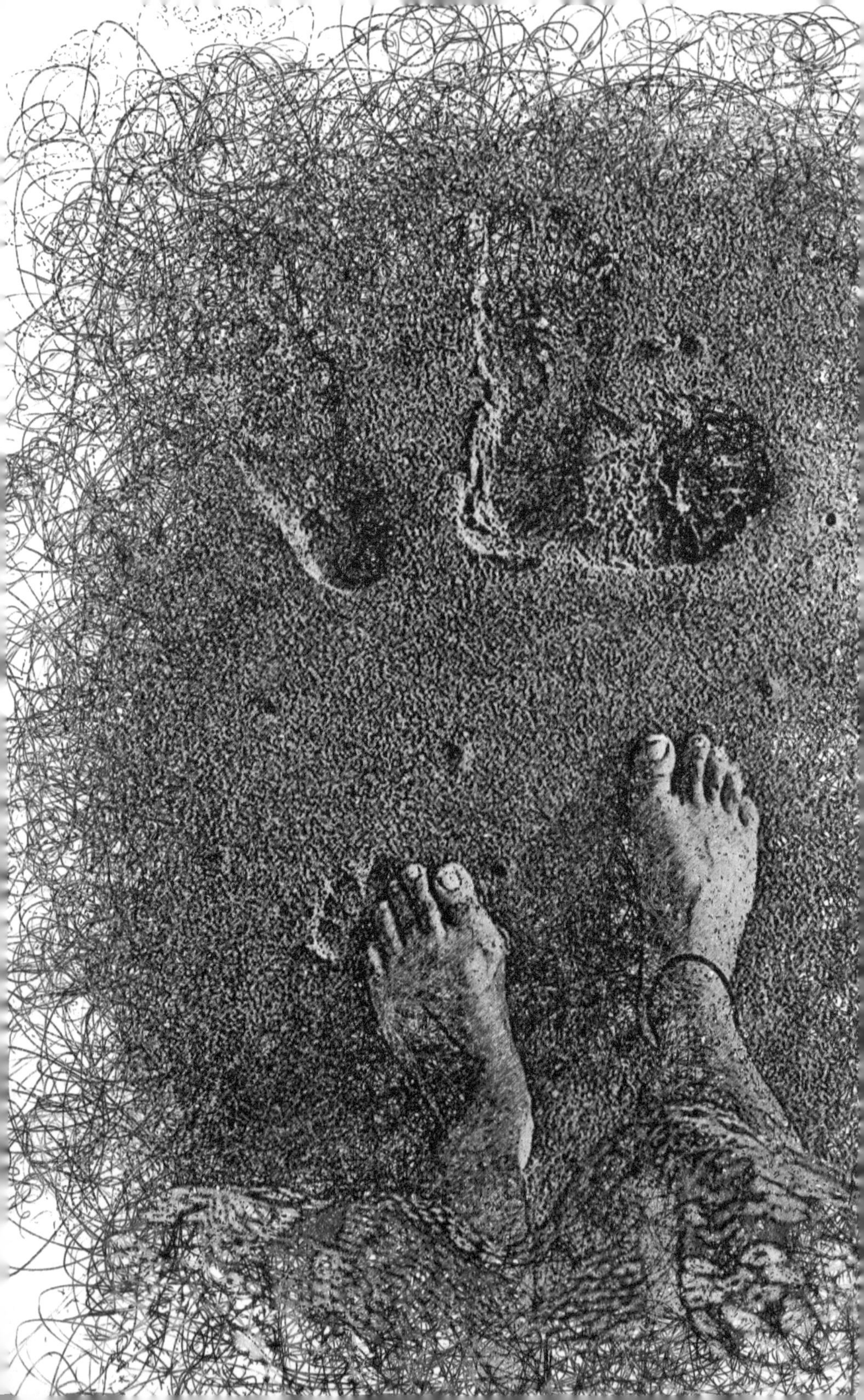

AWAITING

At the door, there!
She spotted none prior.
Seen her weep never.
Her cheer was
among her ones.
At the door, there!
She views one.
Who wishes for
her coming.
To have a being
awaiting
near, away,
is nothing less
a magic.

THEM

The run of subtle pink
that rushed through
her cheeks were
stronger than
her uttered words.
In the West,
the condensing of
the big Star. But,
more pleasurable
it was to sight it
descend through the
reflection in his
Eyes.

SONG OF A LADY-LOVE

'Tis something I looked without an awe.
With me, I have my poesy.
My only virtue.
I know not when.
Let not anyone conquer,
he set his foot into mine.
It striked unto me
that I'm in love.
Thou, taught the art and craft.
Thou kept adding colours to my bouquet
until I, noted, I ain't brave.
This is my first.
To let go may turn dense
after gathering.
Oh! Thoughts…
I arrested myself to his sight.
He has voyages that long
so do I.
To see the end
is our desire and
may I write hymns
on us with the grace of
Polymnia.

HER JOURNEY

Afore the first ring of the alarm
awake was she.
The first tender rays
began to fall on her
through the curtains.
She drew them to view
the young hues of sky
and analyzed it was a morning
of ice and dew.
She was restless to be ready
as the day she dreamt of
approached;
was set for a souvenir.
Quick and unplanned were her ride,
panicking a little thinking of
experiences she might attain.
Indeed a journey to boost
her subconsciousness,
to accomplish strength to
bear boldness.
This was a journey that
answered to

all her questions.
She boarded a city
to never regret.
And that she would recall
each second with the selfsame
liveliness.

APRIL'S REMINDER

April's hatched yellow,
reminds her infant fancy.
Adamant about Grandma to
walk her around wherever.
The merry of gazing stars
in that zephyr cuddling her;
a piece from her drape fails
never to shield her from flu.

ON A WINTER

In the scape of Winter,
amid its bleak winds
they kept dangling in
the other's strength
of warmth.

WORLD POETRY DAY

A solace in goodness,
a solace in dark days.
In allure eves and
heroic crescents,
a being made
garlands of words.
Fulfilled her wholly
that she could only
call it as 'poetry.'

MY DEAREST BLOOM

Shall, at all times, I choose
to be with the late blooms.
The ones in plenty water,
enough Spring still slow
to show lights.

I'm one among them,
I'm them,
we grieve not in delay.
We, hopefully await for
our Seasons of bloom.

TO MY MUSE

When a muse within
sang lullabies of feel,
my pal of art, drizzled
upon the musings to
self reflection.
That ever lingering
gloom was unasked.
The pleasant put at
stillness.
What remains of me
was ordered to be
penned.
To be penned until
was a form of lyrics.

UNDER THE PEEPAL TREE

Before the echoes remain
of the bell, I left.
Walking out of
the mosaic doors,
that kept slapping back and forth.
I sat under the oldest grown
where were bits of ripe twigs,
cawing from nest
and giggling of leaves.
I witnessed the rays leave tan on me.
I witnessed people covered
in the heat of love.
My hair danced along but
there's something, I'm unaware of.
That took me to sleep
in tiredness.
I noticed the leaves noticing
me in distress.
Every time I sobbed,
they eased me.
Surrounded by the humblest.

It’s yet to be found.
They say ‘calm down.’
How can I discard the chaos
of my mind?

ON A MONSOON EVE

Under the light
about to conclude from
last few minutes to day,
infants of moringa
served as den to moths.

Somewhere
I took look at a human
play on the strings.
My chimes too jiggled,
I was unaware of
a musician far nearby…

Through the
silhouettes of conversing
trees aftermath
of a heavy fall was
place for mating birds.

His strings gave an
aura of words,
that were too chaotic
and urged to get out.

Just so when I did
flashes appeared again.
Who such silly it is
to fiddle?
'Thou hath felt the
melody of an unseen man.'
Screamed from in.

The clouds seem to
never leave the sky when
people prepared
for the next mizzle.
I, for a story
to begin anew.

'Twas downpour!
where beings went
silently to sleep.
His melodies reminded
me the melancholy
of previous rain.
Yesterdays scared the
past me.

Who were the two?
One here another there.
Whoever it may be
I watch them in grace.

BIRTH OF A MOTHER

At the onset of January
of the year; towards the
climax of winter is when
she lived through a nameless
trouble.
Never knew until she found out
what kept disrupting awhile.
Several days of sleepless nights
various hours of starving a few
seconds of being breathless;
a la fin, back alive.
A reward offered by universe.
She was born, once again.
Her tender age was
never pampered,
nurtured, cared.
Clueless of how to mother,
in a season
she saw herself
holding a part of

her soul in it; that she
carried in her.
Was quite a day for
remembrance.
A day a mother was born.

TO THE STAR I ONCE ADMIRED

C'est septembre et le ciel est beau.

The september sky is beautiful.
Venus shined than expected.
Stars, brilliant and intense
as I'm.
I was an ordinary with finite reveries
who ambled ignoring the sky.
One day, I was called to gaze,
for a bit only.
Later, inquisitive I was
to have my eyes at the one.
Moonlight bathed in refreshment
which caught the sight of every layman.
Whom I couldn't stop admiring, twinkled
every second; nearest to the biggest star.
Days and weeks went swiftly.
Our conversations; gibberish.
On the day after windstorm,
I took notice of a thing.
The star was gone, to somewhere far.

I thought to run to it but
didn't want to make
myself a clown.
I feel dejected still
of not knowing in accuracy.
From my only star to a star.
Who came with aspirational gifts,
who forced me to fall for dreams,
was instantly gone.
I ain't ready for anything else
than to mourn
for its vanishment.

MOON- A LONGING

You are in every invisible
Pearls I'd hang around.
I detest to jewel stones.
Awaits a day, I, to
embellish my neck of
your kisses.

You made more of
me a feminine than
my bosom or blood.
I beheld the least
to sense intimacy.

You majestically govern
dark, in your absence, I'm
an insomniac.

I see you journey
through more and more.
I stand out the hundreds?
My dry demeanour attracts,
you?

I crippled me to
not again, for a
fall that would
tear all of me.
I'm incapable to
Love.

I trained to
not witness
trusts, embraces.
If I do, I'd carry you
till each of me
becomes ashes.

That night,
I slept me naked
to your lights.
That I know, I'm
insanely, intensely,
in you.

FOR YOU

If the gust gifts
me a handful of
    florets,
I shall preserve
to make a temple
of garlands for you.

MY TRAIN ODYSSEY

Umpteen blinking eyes
and beating hearts.
Diverse, wanderers,
artisans.
Amid them were us-
Two lives I hold onto
and I.
At the brink of
Departure, we bagged in.
The guard shoved his
flag…

It got going with tiny
bumps in increasing
events of rumbling
and booming.
Gifted my eyes were
who a novel to
such sights.

I explored a town
on moors, bushes

and sapling.
I looked over to
shelters and dens.
We're two stops away.

More than many
entered than left.
Many exchanged
glances or a smile,
sharing an eve of
dripping Summer.

I rested my head
at the door in the
slumber inducing
breeze.

Got to our terminal.
One from our lives,
still inside, began
journey to his next
stop.

Our unwavering
hands kept
offering farewell
until its visibility
vanished from us.

SHORE SECRETS

By the shore of the sea
at the eve of horizon,
were more beings than
usual embracing February.

They poured their selves
as they dipped their soles.
They had ardent eyes for
swaying waves.

On the verge held lives
of times different.
A few fancying infancy,
and others thriving.

In those subtle rushes
they were unwavering,
under the glorious, amber
Sunset.

www.ingramcontent.com/pod-product-compliance
Lightning Source LLC
Chambersburg PA
CBHW050025170726
48282CB00025B/552
* 9 7 8 8 1 9 8 1 6 9 0 8 2 *